The Prestige Series

Doncaster 2

Independents - From 1950

Roger Holmes

© 2006 Venture Publications Ltd

ISBN-10: 1 905304 01 3

ISBN-13: 978 1 905304 01 1

Throughout the book, all photographs are by the author unless otherwise stated.

Cover: Two Leyland Atlanteans in the Severn fleet. *(Geoff Coxon)*

Rear cover: Photographed at Doncaster's Christ Church terminus, Felix **37**, **TWR 174**, new in 1957, was the third of eight AEC Regent Vs. It was later fitted with platform doors.

Inside front cover: J H Barras's Don Motors was sold to East Midland in April 1962. **VDT 94**, the 1956 Burlingham-bodied Leyland PD2/20, fitted exactly into the East Midland numbering scheme as D94. Behind it is **EDT 680**, Don's Leyland bodied PD1. **HBE 260**, seen in the lower picture at South Kirkby on a private hire, began life as ABE 961, a Plaxton bodied AEC Regal new to Enterprise and Silver Dawn in 1938, which passed to Lincolnshire Road Car in March 1950. The chassis was lengthened to 30 feet and it reappeared in June 1951 as Lincolnshire 1811, complete with Saunders-Roe 39-seat body. It was later sold to Thompson of Crowle and then, in 1963, to Harold Wilson, where it stayed in service until 1969. It served for many more years as a store shed in Premier's yard.

Inside rear cover: One of the very few Ailsas to be supplied new to independent operators, Premier's **NET 520R** had an Alexander body. It passed through several hands before spending several years in the Wallace Arnold fleet.

Title page: Leon purchased several double-deckers from London Transport, including **BLH 778**, which had been STL 719, in 1954. It stayed just two years with Leon. *(G H F Atkins/© John Banks Collection)*

Below: Morgan & Store may have been unique in having Guy Arabs of Marks I, II, III, IV and V in service at the same time. This 1965 shot, posed in Stainforth, shows **FTD 69**, **FPT 205**, **LWR 337**, **SWU 873** and **CWW 399B**.

>> Opposite page: Rossie's **220 AWY** was just three months old when photographed in September 1962. Unusual because it was a CVD6/30, it has survived into preservation, initially with South Yorks PTE.

ACKNOWLEDGEMENTS

I am greatly indebted to all those fellow enthusiasts who have helped in the preparation of this book, to Mike Fowler for checking the draft, to Roy Marshall for corrections and some useful additional information, and to Tony Peart, whose painstaking study of the text brought to light some matters which ought to be made clearer and who was able to update a number of items.

Aiden Proctor and Jim Sambrooks have been most generous with their assistance over, among other things, the activities of Leon Motors and Wilfreda-Beehive in the current, ever-changing era. As a result, after possessing too little information, I have now more than I could possibly use. Bob Rowe, too, has been a great help with some of my enquiries.

My thanks also to the Series Editor, John Banks, for his cheerful encouragement and technical expertise.

Roger Holmes,
Stalybridge, December 2005

INTRODUCTION

This book continues the story of Doncaster's independent operators begun in the companion book *"Doncaster 1, Independents - The First 30 Years"*. It picks up the thread in 1950, when the dust had settled after the problems and privations of the Second World War and the make do and mend necessary then and in the years of austerity and rationing immediately following.

At the beginning of the 1950s the pattern of operation of the independents' services into Doncaster was well established, largely based on the prewar model. To the east, from Doncaster to Thorne Moorends on the "Top Road", weekdays saw a half-hourly headway, provided by T Severn & Sons, Felix Motors and Harold Wilson's Premier. The Dunscroft route via Stainforth was shared among Doncaster Corporation, Severn and Samuel Morgan Ltd (Blue Line) and its associated company R Store Ltd (Reliance), with Severn operating the market day service to Fishlake and Sykehouse, which had come from W Roe just before the war. Morgan & Store's hourly

service to Goole was a stand alone, no longer integrated with the Dunscroft route, though sharing the same road as far as Stainforth, and Reliance went through rural parts to Kirkhouse Green every Saturday. Felix Motors, Morgan's Blue Line and the Corporation worked the Armthorpe service jointly every 15 minutes.

Timings to Rossington seemed set in stone, with the Corporation leaving Doncaster on the hour, G H Ennifer Ltd (Blue Ensign) at 15 minutes past, Rossie Motors on the half hour and Don Motors (J H Barras) at a quarter to the hour. Leon Motors had only just assimilated the business of Thomas Madeley (another Premier) from Blaxton, whose six buses all joined the Leon fleet. The overall timetable between Doncaster to Finningley, Blaxton, Wroot and Misson was little changed. E R Dodd's Selwyn Motors came in from Belton on market days, as did Thomas Holling from Moss and Fenwick.

Generally, 1951 found these operators in a healthy position. Business on the services was booming; there was little private motoring and petrol was only just becoming freely available. Only a few prewar vehicles remained in stock and many of these would be withdrawn during the course of the year. Most of the routes to the east and south of the town were almost exclusively worked by double-deckers, with the exception of the market day services and that to Goole, on which double-deckers could not be used.

Double-deckers had yet to appear on the Wakefield service, which ran on an hourly headway, with the three firms concerned, working as the United Service, rotating their timings on a complicated 15-week rota. Cooper Brothers had only single-deckers, and the very few double-deckers owned by W R & P Bingley and W Everett & Sons worked around South Kirkby and Hemsworth.

As housing development began in the 1950s, some routes saw alterations and additions. The Rossington service was augmented by a short working to Church Lane via Bessacarr on four days a week, replaced in 1973 by a service to West Bessacarr. All the four operators concerned held a licence for this, but in practice it was run by Doncaster Corporation. Rossie Motors began to provide a different route through Rossington village, using West End Lane.

Above: An experimental vehicle, designated TV45/2, from the period when Daimler were developing the CVD6 range. Willowbrook bodied **FRW 587** was a Daimler company works bus before being sold to Kitchens of Pudsey. It arrived with Leon in 1955 and stayed for seven years.

Below: Not many independents used the Leyland Royal Tiger with Leyland coach body on service work. **KWY 903** was one of a pair delivered to W R & P Bingley in May 1952, and is shown here in the depressing surroundings of Doncaster's Marshgate bus station.

Doncaster to Thorne Moorends was in effect two routes, one going direct from Hatfield to Thorne (styled "via Brickyards"), the other going through Hatfield Woodhouse. The large South Common estate was built in the early 1960s, and the route via Brickyards was diverted to serve this, finally running through the estate when the roads were completed. All three concerns on this route shared these, together with a service to Lindholme Aerodrome.

In 1953 the Dunscroft terminus was moved further, from the Broadway Hotel to Ingram Road, and somewhat later in Armthorpe the route split to terminate at either Mercel Avenue or Eastfield Road. Later still the delightful destination of "Cow House Lane" could be seen.

Thorne Colliery closed in 1956 because of flooding, and the National Coal Board made arrangements for the miners to be transferred to other collieries in the area. Doncaster Corporation and several independents gained contracts to provide works services from Thorne Moorends to pits at Bentley, Brodsworth, Hatfield Main, Rossington and Yorkshire Main. As shifts were involved this was virtually a round the clock operation, and had a significant effect on vehicle policy.

Owners naturally jealously guarded their share of the routes, and when services were altered or additional journeys proved necessary it led to increasingly complex joint arrangements. As an example, here is the agreement as it was in 1974 for the Doncaster to Thorne Moorends service:

"Monday to Friday - five duties.

Each operator provides one bus all day: one bus shared by all three operators on an eight-week cycle ("J" service) and operated by Felix Motors and T Severn & Sons for three weeks each and by H Wilson for two weeks out of every eight: one bus shared by Felix Motors and T Severn & Sons and operated on alternate weeks by each operator except for the two weeks when H Wilson operates the "J" service when it is operated alternately start to mid afternoon and mid afternoon to finish by each of the two operators.

Saturday - seven duties.

Felix Motors and T Severn & Sons each provide two buses all day: H Wilson provides one bus all day; one is shared by Felix Motors and T Severn & Sons and operated alternately start to mid afternoon and mid afternoon to finish on alternate weeks; one bus is operated morning by Felix Motors and T Severn & Sons for three months each out of every six and by H Wilson afternoon and evening throughout the year.

Sunday as Monday to Friday except that the bus shared by Felix Motors and T Severn & Sons is operated by each firm on alternate weeks throughout the year."

The above is a simplified version of the agreement, which provides for some diversions via Lindholme Aerodrome and additional journeys between Doncaster and Lindholme on a "J" service basis with extra trips operated by Felix Motors.

The joint services to Dunscroft, Armthorpe, Rossington and Wakefield all had similar, if not perhaps quite so involved, agreements. Any one wishing to study these in detail is recommended to the Omnibus Society Publication, *"Joint Operation in South Yorkshire. A survey of the situation in March 1974"*, from which the above extract was taken. Needless to say when the PTE began acquiring businesses piecemeal the arrangements were a headache for scheduling staff, not least the notorious "J" service. The independents could cover these "rotating" turns with part-time and other staff, but there were problems for the more formalised duty rosters.

It was interesting to see how vehicle policy reflected owners' personal preferences and the desire to be different. It was possible, when travelling to Rossington, to compare Rossie's Daimlers, Don's Leylands and Blue Ensign's Crossley or AECs under similar conditions. Likewise Severn's Leylands, Felix's AECs and Morgan & Store's Guy Arabs all ran from the Christ Church terminus. What a field day some of today's bus journalists would have had. With the advent of the rear engine though, they all took to the Daimler Fleetline with the exception of Severn, still flying the flag for Leyland with Atlanteans.

Above: One of a number of Bedford VAL coaches in the Morgan & Store consortium, **AWT 351B** was often used to transport miners from Thorne Moorends to other collieries in the district.

Below: Although Severns were primarily users of Leylands, in 1956 they took a pair of AEC Reliances bodied by Park Royal with coach seats. **PYG 605** is seen at the Dunscroft premises.

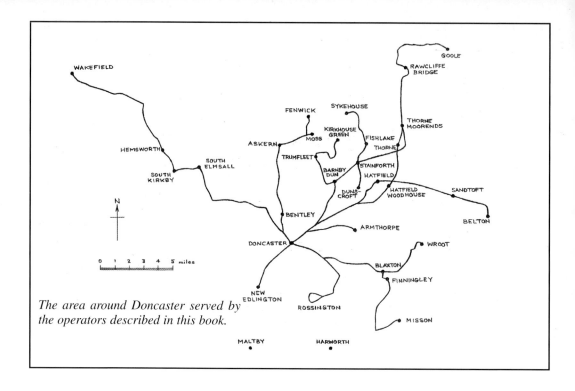

The area around Doncaster served by the operators described in this book.

D S Hellewell's book *"South Yorkshire's Transport 1974 to 1995"* (Venture Publications, 1996) gives annual figures for stage mileage for the year ending 31st March 1976:

Blue Ensign	104,985
Felix	334,911
Leon	256,033
Rossie	100,391
S Morgan	348,891
R Store	274,382
T Severn	399,172
W R & P Bingley	241,655
Cooper Bros	97,971
H Wilson	155,086

When the South Yorkshire PTE was established in 1974 it found itself with a duty laid down in the Transport Act of 1968 to integrate public passenger transport throughout the county. The independent operators felt threatened, especially in view of publicly expressed statements made by certain, mostly Sheffield, councillors from "The People's Republic of South Yorkshire". Nor did they believe that their localised services could be properly run from headquarters miles away in

Sheffield. They were suspicious, and it took several meetings with PTE representatives before good relationships were established and it was possible to thrash out schemes for standard fares and conditions, concessions for pensioners and children and compensatory payments.

It was made clear that the PTE was not intending to apply pressure on companies to sell out - how could they? However, transport policy could be implemented much more easily if services were under their overall control. A key factor, and doubtless the PTE was well aware of it, was that hardly any of the original busmen were still alive, and many of their successors were coming up to retirement age. The companies, still trading profitably, were now in the hands of the shareholders, some second or third generation, some of whom were not particularly interested in buses and could find other uses for their money. Although one or two of the early negotiations fell through, it was felt that most of the independents would sell out "if the price was right". And so it proved.

By the end of the 1980s only Leon, with its sizeable Excursion and Tours and Private Hire connection, and routes which ran partly out of

Above: Felix **42**, **8176 WY**, an AEC Regent V, although 15 years old, was still immaculate when pictured passing Lindholme Aerodrome on the last day of Felix operation. *(Jim Sambrooks)*

Below: **LWT 704**, a Harrington-bodied Daimler Freeline, was the flagship of Everett's fleet when it came from Kitchens of Pudsey in 1956. It is shown here at Doncaster races.

South Yorkshire territory, together with Selwyn Motors' tiny operation, remained.

OPERATORS NORTH OF DONCASTER

United Service on the Wakefield Route

This was an association of operators which was set up in November 1926 to operate the Doncaster to Wakefield route and serve the mining communities of South Elmsall, South Kirkby and Hemsworth. Originally there were four participants, but Newsholme Brothers sold out to the others in 1933. Tickets issued by the partners were identical, distinguished by the base colour only. Cooper's were yellow, Everett's white and Granter's blueish green. Buses carried a similar livery of turquoise and blue, with some displaying "United Service" and sometimes an owner's emblem. At first the Doncaster terminus was in the concrete "outrigger" from the North Bridge, shared with the Bentley trolleybuses and routes to Leeds, Askern, Skellow, Woodlands, etc. This proved far too small, and West Riding, South Yorkshire, Bullock & Sons, United Service and Holling were banished to the dismal and inconvenient Marshgate bus station for many years.

W Everett & Son

At the beginning of 1950 Everett's fleet consisted of two Dennis Lancet 2s with Dennis bodies, two Daimler CVD6s and CK 4433, an elderly Leyland TD1 with Gardner 5LW engine. Both Dennises and the TD1 rapidly departed to be replaced by a Plaxton-bodied Foden, an AEC Regal and an ex-Barrow Daimler CWG5.

The following 18 years saw a bewildering selection of vehicles come and go, 42 in total, with just two - a Burlingham-bodied Atkinson CPL44 and a Bedford SB - bought new.

Fifteen were double-deckers: three Guy Arab 2s, an Arab 3, two Daimler CWA6s, two Bristol K5Gs, an ex-London STL, an AEC Regent III, a Leyland PD1, three PD2s and a Dennis Loline 1. Single-deckers were no less varied: an AEC Regal IV, eight Reliances, an Albion Valkyrie, a Daimler Freeline D650H, a Crossley, three Leyland PS1s and a PS2, two

Royal Tiger PSU1s, two Beadle-Leylands, four Bedford SBs and a Ford Thames. As will be imagined, few stayed long in the fleet. The firm operated from a depot on the main Barnsley Road in South Kirkby, where passers-by were assured of seeing something fresh.

Latterly the name became William & Harry Everett, t/a W Everett & Son, and it was never formed into a limited company. It was sold, together with Everett's share of the United Services operation (Doncaster - Wakefield and Hemsworth - Wakefield) to W R & P Bingley in November 1969. Four vehicles went to Bingleys: Bedford SB5 Duple 94 DWT, Bristol K5G JUO 918, Guy Arab 3 HWO 328 and the Dennis Loline SOU 473.

Following this sale, Bingleys held 11/15ths of the United Service operation, and Cooper Brothers 4/15ths. The service pattern was quite involved: there were three duties rotating on a 15-week cycle. For four out of five weeks Bingley had two and Cooper one. On week five Bingleys ran all three. At peak times Monday to Friday additional buses ran on a similar rota between Hemsworth and Wakefield. On Saturdays two buses ran between South Elmsall and Wakefield. These were worked by Bingley four weeks out of every five, the fifth week was operated by Coopers, and was the week in which Coopers had no bus running from Doncaster.

Cooper Brothers

Coopers' was never a large operation, and much of the service driving for many years was done by the brothers Lawrence Lee Cooper and Walter Lee Cooper. The fleet never exceeded four buses, and the two faithful Maudslays, an ML3 and a later Marathon, which had borne the brunt of heavy war-time loadings, just lasted into the 1950s. They were replaced by a Plaxton-bodied Daimler CVD6 and JTB 749, an AEC Regal III with Burlingham body which survives in preservation, albeit in its original Florence Motors livery.

Another CVD6 joined later from Kitchen of Pudsey. When double-deck operation became possible, MDT 220, an AEC Regent III Roe, was bought from Doncaster Corporation, who were disposing of their lowbridge vehicles, having no further use for them. During its

Above: Although Manchester Corporation never got on with their Leyland Panther Cubs, Cooper Brothers were quite satisfied with **ANF 161B**, which gave them years of front-line service. *(Mike Fowler)*

Below: Cooper's first double-decker was **MDT 220**, bought in 1959 when Doncaster Corporation had no further use for lowbridge vehicles. The AEC Regent III was withdrawn in September 1971 and replaced by the Panther Cub.

twelve-year stay with the Coopers it visited the Doncaster garage at Leicester Avenue for maintenance and testing. None of the three double-decks which followed, a PD1 and 2 PD2s, all from Ribble, lasted as long with the South Kirkby concern.

During the mid 1970s the service was run by two Willowbrook-bodied Bedfords, a VAM70 and a YRQ, both bought new, together with ANF 161B, an ex-Manchester Panther Cub. All were very smartly kept. It is interesting that, contrary to Manchester's experience, Coopers thought well of their Panther Cub, which gave them very little trouble.

The Cooper business was sold to W R & P Bingley on 3rd April 1977, just two weeks before the West Yorkshire PTE acquired Bingley's undertaking.

W R & P Bingley

G W Bingley started his business in 1921 with a 14-seat Ford. During the years which followed, William Reginald Bingley continued operations from the base at Kinsley, his daughter Phyllis later joining the company. They ran a short stage service from South Kirkby to Frickley, together with contract and private hire, all of which are outside the scope of this book.

In June 1949, however, the Bingleys bought the business of John Joseph Granter, the largest partner in the United Service group. With this came shares in the Doncaster - Wakefield and Hemsworth to Wakefield routes, together with premises in Upton. The vehicles involved included a Gardner-engined Leyland Lion LT5A, two Daimler COG5s, an ex-Sheffield TD4 Titan and four Daimler CVD6s - two Duple coaches and two Willowbrook-bodied buses. The Lion and the TD4 soon went, being replaced by a Daimler COG6 from Bradford and an ex-Leeds Leyland TD5.

Modernisation of the coaching side proceeded apace with two Leyland-bodied PSU1 coaches, two AEC Regal IVs bodied by Yeates, followed by a Burlingham Seagull body on the Daimler D650H Freeline chassis, all new. Double-deckers bought included an ex-LPTB Daimler CWA6 and LTO 10, a handsome Duple-bodied Daimler CVD6, from

Skills of Nottingham. In 1957 a pair of brand new double-deckers arrived, AEC Regent Vs with lowbridge Roe bodies. Further new coaches comprised three AEC Reliances, three Leyland Leopards and two Bedfords.

There was a Strachan dual-purpose bodied AEC Reliance which had been a demonstrator, and a Leyland Leopard with Plaxton dual-purpose body. A Bedford SB came from the Ministry of Defence and, unusually for an independent, there was SWT 704F, an AEC Swift with bus body by Willowbrook.

As mentioned earlier, four vehicles came with the Everett business in 1969. The Bristol K5G was not used, and the other three did not stay long.

The Cooper business passed to Bingley at the beginning of April 1977, and a fortnight later the whole service passed to the West Yorkshire PTE, and with it the whole of the Doncaster to Wakefield route, plus much of the traffic in South Elmsall, South Kirkby and Hemsworth, although Yorkshire Traction did have a presence in the area. For a considerable time West Yorkshire operated Upton as a separate unit. Transferred to the PTE were at least four Leopards, two Reliances, two Bedford coaches and the Swift.

T W Holling

Thomas Walter Holling of Belmont Garage, Askern, was the old-established operator of a Saturdays-only service from Moss and Fenwick, which terminated in Doncaster's squalid Marshgate bus station. In 1950 he owned two Bedfords: an OWB and an OB Duple Vista, both bought new, and an ex-Barton Duple-bodied Leyland PS1. A period of expansion into private hire work began in the 1950s. Another OB followed, and a petrol-engined Albion Victor with Duple coachwork, which gave 18 years of service. A Beadle-bodied OB and a forward-control Morris Commercial with Wadham body were soon sold, though a rebodied Daimler CVD6 from Fieldsend was kept much longer.

More new vehicles came in the 1950s in the shape of two Bedford SBs, an AEC Reliance and a Plaxton-bodied Albion Aberdonian, and a further Albion Victor, with a Scottish Aviation body, joined the fleet.

Above: For several years **KWU 462**, a petrol-engined Albion Victor with Duple bodywork, was a regular perfomer on Hollings Saturday service to Moss and Fenwick. It is seen here loading in Marshgate, where the route was never allocated a proper stand.

Below: **LJW 336**, a Saunders-Roe-bodied Guy Arab LUF, worked as a Guy demonstrator for two years before passing to Blue Line in 1955. It was withdrawn at the end of 1964, becoming a store shed in Stainforth, but was subsequently rescued for preservation.

The following decade saw more interesting new stock: an AEC Reliance Duple Midland, an Albion VT21L with Duple Northern Firefly body, two Bedford VAM14s and a Bristol LH coach. WJU 406, a Leyland Leopard L2, was an ex-Willowbrook demonstrator, while another ex-demonstrator was a Bedford VAS1 with an extended chassis. Second-hand were a pair of Reliances, a Bedford VAS and a YRQ, while in the 1970s a Ford R192 and a Bedford SB5 were added.

The Saturdays-only service ceased in August 1967, but Holling's coaching activities continued for some years after that.

OPERATORS EAST OF DONCASTER

Samuel Morgan Ltd (Blue Line)

One of the pioneers on the service to Stainforth, and later to Goole, was Samuel Morgan. Towards the end of the 1920s he was not in the best of health and wanted to sell the business. Robert Store, whose operations paralleled his, hoped to buy it, but was thwarted by Doncaster Corporation, who refused to transfer the licences. A limited company, Samuel Morgan Ltd, had been formed and Richard Wilson, who ran as Blue Line on the Armthorpe route, bought the company and transferred his own licence to it, changing the fleet name from Gwen to his own Blue Line. Samuel's son Cliff remained as a driver for many years.

In April 1949 Robert Store retired, and his Reliance business also came into the Wilson fold. A holding company, Morgan & Store Ltd, was set up, but the two concerns were run separately, though operations on the Stainforth - Dunscroft - Goole corridor dovetailed well. Richard Wilson remained in charge of the Blue Line affairs at Armthorpe, while his brother John ran the Reliance concern in Stainforth. The Stainforth joinery firm of Cauldwell was bought at this time and renamed Wilson Cauldwell, the workshops being used for body repairs and maintenance. Store's unusual pale green and cream livery with dark blue band was retained until vehicles were repainted. His final order, a second Barnaby-bodied Leyland Comet, was actually delivered more than a year after the takeover, and was the last to carry these colours.

New vehicles were delivered carrying Blue Line or Reliance fleet names in gold, but on repainting these were not replaced. A standard style was adopted. Blue Line buses were predominantly mid-dark blue with pale blue relief, while Reliance used the same two shades reversed.

The Wilsons were among the numerous operators impressed by the rugged simplicity and economy of their wartime Guy Arabs, and for many years all double- and most single-deckers purchased were Guys. By 1950 they already had, in addition to the three Arab IIs, a pair of Arab IIIs with Guy bodies and Meadows engines which, like others fitted with this power unit, had Gardner units fitted on first overhaul. At that time some of the older, more eccentric stock had gone, but possibly due to the re-engining and rebodying programme undertaken in the 1940s six prewar vehicles remained: two of the lightweight Gilford PF166s and a rebodied 168OT, two re-engined Daimler CF6s, the Foden and a TSM Express.

All were withdrawn fairly quickly, only the wartime rebodied TSM soldiered on until 1954. Replacements were second-hand Guy Arab III saloons with assorted bodies by Barnard, Thurgood and Massey.

In May 1953 the stage carriage services of Hopley & Richardson (Majestic) of Thorne were taken over. At the time these were Stainforth (Fox Inn) to Goole and a colliery run between Thorne Moorends and Hatfield Main pit. This meant that Morgan & Store now had a monopoly of services between Doncaster and Goole. Two Sentinel-Beadle 40 seaters, both ex-demonstrators, came with the deal, and ran for a couple of years in Majestic's red and cream livery. After withdrawal in December 1955, GUJ 457 languished in the yard for a year before returning to service in December 1956 painted blue, running for a further year.

Majestic's coaching interests ended in February 1964, when their three petrol-engined Bedford SBs were taken over by Harold Wilson's Premier. Incidentally Richardson, the active partner, had been a driver for Store before launching out on his own in 1929.

A new era began in the mid 1950s when it became possible to run larger capacity vehicles to Goole. There was a Leyland Tiger Cub in 1954 and a Guy Arab LUF in 1955, with

Above: Blue Line took over the Majestic service and with it two ex-demonstrator Sentinel-Beadles in December 1953. **GNT 587** is pictured five months later still in its red and cream Majestic livery.

Below: "Yogi" was the nickname of the Roe-bodied Guy Arab IV **7014 YG**. New in 1962, it was the only Guy in the Blue Line fleet with a Johannesburg-style front, and is pictured here at Roe's Crossgates Carriage Works.

similar Mann Egerton bodies, followed by a stylish Burlingham bus-bodied Arab LUF.

The Mulliner-bodied Meadows-engined Guy Warrior bought in 1957, besides looking ugly, proved troublesome and was sold. A notable purchase was LJW 336, an ex-demonstrator and another LUF, with a Saunders-Roe body of similar pattern to those supplied to several BET companies on Tiger Cub chassis. On withdrawal it became a store shed at Stainforth and survives in preservation.

An exhibit at the 1956 Commercial Motor Show was another milestone in the company's history. SWU 876 was a Burlingham-bodied Guy Arab IV, the first 30ft-long double-decker in the Doncaster area. As usual on overhaul its Meadows engine was replaced by a Gardner 6LW, though a second similar Arab delivered in 1959 was Gardner-powered from new. Four more 30ft Arabs came in the 1960s, this time bodied by Charles H Roe. One of these, a Mark 4 with Johannesburg-style bonnet and grille was 7014 YG, naturally known to staff as "Yogi". The other three were of the Mark V variety. Second-hand double-deckers bought were an ex-Sunderland Arab II rebodied by Roe and FTD 69, an Arab I from Lancaster Corporation, which had been rebodied by Guy in 1963. At one time the Blue Line fleet contained examples of Guy Arabs of Marks I, II, III, IV and V - surely unique. It has been reported that at some stage Richard Wilson was interested in the Guy Wulfrunian, but fortunately thought better of the idea. For 25 years all double-deck purchases had been Guys, but in 1968 a brace of three-year-old Leyland PD3 Titans with Roe bodies came from the Kippax & District fleet.

As mentioned in the introduction, Thorne Colliery closed in 1956 as a result of persistent flooding, and the miners employed there, mostly living in the Thorne Moorends area, had to be transported to other pits. Doncaster Corporation and several independents provided transport on a round-the-clock basis, and Blue Line and Reliance were heavily involved. They both held licences from Thorne Moorends to Bentley, Brodsworth, Hatfield Main, Yorkshire Main and Rossington Collieries. A succession of coaches was employed in this work, 23 in this fleet alone, almost all bought new and painted in a cream and pale blue livery. There

were Bedfords of various types, including four VALs, supplemented latterly by Fords. In addition Excursion & Tours licences were held from Armthorpe and Stainforth.

The Fleetline era began in 1971 when two were delivered, another following in 1975 and a further pair in 1977, all bodied by Roe. Driver-only operation began in the early 1970s, although the Willebrew system was still in use on crewed buses until the PTE takeover. TIMs were also used at Armthorpe.

Richard Wilson died in November 1974 while still active in the business at the age of 74. His brother John then became Managing Director of Blue Line, with John's son Tony taking over the Reliance operation in Stainforth. On John's death four years later Tony took over the reins of both concerns.

The two companies were sold to the South Yorkshire PTE in March 1979 for a reported £400,000. The following day T Severn & Sons sold out, with their modern premises in Dunscroft becoming a base for operations east of Doncaster, and Morgan & Store vehicles were transferred there, with the Armthorpe and Stainforth premises subsequently being sold.

Cliff Theaker, operations manager in Armthorpe, joined the PTE, as did most of the staff. He had been secretary to the Thorne Road group of independent operators and had a store of useful information at his fingertips. At the takeover two Dennis Dominators with East Lancs bodies were on order and these, with certain alterations to the specification, were delivered to the PTE in due course.

R Store Ltd (Reliance)

It is scarcely surprising that there are many similarities between the post 1950 activities of R Store Ltd and the parent company S Morgan Ltd. They shared timings on the Doncaster - Dunscroft and the Doncaster - Goole routes, though Store never ran to Armthorpe. Both participated in the conveyance of miners from Thorne Moorends to other pits, but Store also had a works service from Dunscroft to Burton's tailoring factory in Goole. There was a Saturdays-only rural service too which threaded its way to Kirkhouse Green via several small villages, and survived until June 1971. The early 1950s found most of Store's

Above: Not quite what it seems: **CDT 186** began life in 1942 as a Massey-bodied Guy Arab 1 of Doncaster Corporation. In 1948 it was rebodied as a coach by Plaxton for Kildare Coaches of Adwick-le-Street, passing to Store in 1952.

Below: Pictured in Kirkhouse Green, **942 AWR** was one if the earliest of the five Bedford SBs with Yeates Pegasus conversions operated by Store.

prewar fleet still in service. There were the AEC Reliance and the Dennis Lancet, both Gardner-powered, a Leyland Cheetah LZ2 and a pretty little Dennis Falcon. A wartime Guy Arab II, a Bedford OB Mulliner and an old ex-Burton Guy single-decker had been joined by a Meadows-engined Guy Arab III with a Barnaby double-deck body. Barnaby bodies were favoured by many Yorkshire independents; they offered no-nonsense service buses and a stylish dual-purpose body, usually soundly built. Their foray into double-deckers after the war was not so happy. The conclusion is that they had studied Roe bodies which had come into the Hull works for repair, but perhaps because of lack of experience or possibly difficulty in obtaining suitable timber at that time, Barnaby built bodies were not so long lasting as the Leeds product. The AEC Reliance and the old ex-Burton Guy went quickly, and the Bedford and the Dennis Falcon (which had gained a Perkins P6 engine) were sold. The Lancet lasted longer as did the Leyland LZ2 which, with its Stainforth-built Barras body, was sold to a farmer in 1954. Store's final order was for two Barnaby-bodied Leyland Comets which arrived after the take-over and proved most useful on the Goole route. Various second-hand Guy Arab single-deckers followed: a Duple-, a Plaxton-, a Lawton- and a Massey-bodied one from Newcastle, together with CDT 186 which had begun life as a Doncaster Corporation Arab I double-decker that had been fitted with a new Plaxton coach body in 1949. Following the parent company's lead, TYG 4 was a 30ft-long Burlingham-bodied Arab IV and there were two second-hand Guys: a rebodied Arab II ex-Sunderland and an NCB-bodied Arab III from Trent. Fifteen coaches - eleven Bedfords and four Fords - came and went, but perhaps the most interesting Bedfords were five with the Yeates Pegasus conversion to front entrances, intended for stage-carriage work. One of these, 998 CWR, was exhibited at the 1962 Commercial Motor Show, while another ended up as Mexborough & Swinton's No. 115. Three Roe bodied Guy Arab Vs arrived in the 1970s; apart from the lettering they were identical in specification and livery to the Morgan ones. They were followed in the next decade by a succession of five Daimler Fleetlines.

In March 1979 the PTE took over the Reliance operation, together with the parent company. Thus ended almost 50 years of what had been an interesting, slightly different, firm which had sported a fascinating selection of vehicles.

From the two companies the PTE took over ten Daimler Fleetlines, two Leyland Titan PD3s, six Bedfords and eight Fords. Five Guy Arab Vs were owned, two of which were out of use. Shortly before the take-over, incredibly, two of the serviceable Guys were written off on the same afternoon when they both ran off the road in the same spot. The one remaining was the oldest of the five, and did not last long with the PTE.

T Severn & Sons

By 1931 Thomas Severn had built up his Cressy fleet to ten vehicles, which made his firm the largest independent in the area, operating on two prime routes: Doncaster - Stainforth (later Dunscroft) and Doncaster - Thorne Moorends. The fleetname Cressy, dropped in wartime, derived from his native Cresswell in Derbyshire. The Severn business was built up with Leylands, together with some lightweight vehicles in the 1920s, but now and then other makes did appear.

The prewar fleet had almost gone by 1950. One Leyland LT7 and an AEC Regal 4 went in January, with a recently rebodied LT7 being sold the following year. Equally ruthless was the culling of the three Massey-bodied Guy Arab IIs. One went in 1950, one in 1951 and the earliest, which had been rebodied, was sold the following year. Already two Leyland PD1 Titans, one Roe and one NCB (later rebodied by Roe) and three Leyland-bodied PD2s had joined the fleet, together with two Barnaby-bodied Leyland PS1s and two more PS1s with Yeates coach bodies. Fleet modernisation was complete by September 1951 with the delivery of three more PD2s and a Royal Tiger PSU1 Duple coach.

Things slowed down in the years which followed; after another PD2, two Park Royal-bodied dual-purpose AEC Reliances appeared and then the first of the 30ft-long double-deckers - a pair of PD3s with Roe bodies. The next two Leyland/Roe PD3 Titans had front

Above: The last of Severn's half-cab double-deckers, Leyland PD3 **BWW 654B**, was new in 1964. It passed to South Yorks PTE in March 1979, was converted into a towing vehicle and as such enjoyed a long life. In the background are two members of Severn's Dunscroft Haulage fleet.

Below: The first of Severn's numerous Leyland Atlanteans came in the following year. **GWX 553C**, with its attractive Roe body, is seen arriving in Doncaster.

entrances, and in the early 1960s came some unusual second-hand acquisitions: a Yeates-bodied Bedford SB and a Leyland Tiger Cub Burlingham together with ex-London Transport RT331 and a Bristol K5G from Brighton, Hove & District. Doubtless there was a reason for buying the last two, but they didn't remain in the fleet for very long.

The Atlantean era began in 1965 with GWX 553C, the first of ten with either Roe or Alexander bodies. Noteworthy was the second of these, delivered in 1969, which had been added to an order for Glasgow, and was the only Albion-badged Atlantean south of the border. A dual-purpose AEC Reliance and three Bedford coaches joined the fleet in later years. Excursion and Tours licences from Stainforth were held, and works services ran from Dunscroft to the Rockware works at Kirk Sandall and to Crompton Road in Doncaster. The buses were invariably smartly kept and instantly recognisable in their consistent shades of green and cream, with latterly a garter badge. TIM ticket-issuing equipment replaced the Bell Punch system in 1953.

In March 1954 Severn moved from cramped premises at Cressy House in Silver Street, Stainforth, to a new purpose-built garage in Bootham Lane, Dunscroft, which was officially opened by the Traffic Commissioner, Major Eastwood. This was surrounded by land and had also at one time been used for a small lorry fleet belonging to Severn: Dunscroft Haulage. The site was of great interest to the PTE and passed into their ownership, with the company, in March 1979, one day after the acquisition of Morgan & Store, although the concern continued as an operating entity until August 1980. A large area of hard standing was created and the Blue Line and Reliance vehicles accommodated, with Colin Fowlston, from Severn, as Operations Manager.

All ten Atlanteans passed into PTE ownership, plus the dual-purpose AEC Reliance, the three Bedfords and a Land Rover. They also took Severn's three surviving front entrance PD3s, which were converted into recovery vehicles and as such enjoyed a very long life.

Felix Motors Ltd

Ernest Parish began his operations, like many others, from East Lane, Stainforth, working between Doncaster and Armthorpe, subsequently adding the route to Thorne Moorends (which Felix alone persistently called Thorne New Village for many years). Parish never served Stainforth, and in 1930 his headquarters moved to a purpose built depot in Park Lane, Dunsville, just to the west of Hatfield. Earlier vehicles carried a Felix the Cat emblem, but later the name Felix Motors Ltd was carried in gold lettering, until a garter badge came into use in 1960. The livery for most of the company's existence was maroon, crimson and cream, and buses were always immaculately turned out. Of the prewar stock remaining in 1950, the year saw the withdrawal of the Gardner-engined Leyland LT7, the ex-South Wales AEC Regent and the Regal coach which had been rebodied as a double-decker, leaving just an elderly Regal which lasted a couple more years, the splendid Leyland TS7 and CWY 758, the pioneer AEC Regent which was sold to Skills of Nottingham in 1955. On disposal almost all Felix buses went to further owners, some for many more years.

Wartime additions were just two: one unfrozen Leyland TD7 and a Roe-bodied Daimler CWA6, which was perhaps unique in being later fitted with an AEC crash gearbox, and then followed an early Leyland PD1 and an NCB-bodied AEC Regent. Next came fleet number 26, the magnificent AEC Regent III with Roberts body, together with two Barnaby-bodied coaches, an AEC Regal III and a Leyland PS1. Nineteen-fifty saw the advent of two more Tiger PS1s with Barnaby coachwork, and a pair of PD2s with Leyland bodies. A fully fronted PS1 coach followed, after which the pendulum swung towards AEC. In the 1950s came two Roe-bodied Regent IIIs, with a total of four Mark Vs coming later; the latter subsequently had platform doors fitted. Two Reliances with Roe Dalesman bodies were added to stock, plus a further example with Roe dual-purpose bodywork, 9629 WU, which has survived into preservation, smart as ever. When Felix coaches were put away in the garage, sheets of paper were laid on the floors to protect them from dirty footmarks. Unlike

Above: Felix No. **33** (**LWY 942**), a Roe-bodied AEC Regent III, was just nine days old when this picture was taken in May 1953. In November 1966 it went for further service to Steele (A1) of Stevenston.

Below: AEC Reliance/Plaxton **VWT 355F** looked ready for its tour of the Bulb Fields when seen at the depot in May 1969.

other local operators at that time Felix never used forward-entrance double-deckers and the four 30ft AEC Regent Vs that entered service in the 1960s all had rear platform doors. Three more Reliance coaches were added to the fleet, a Duple and two Plaxtons.

The first Daimler Fleetline, with bodywork by Roe, arrived in 1969. This was a dual-doorway example, but the following three all had the single-door layout.

Felix had numerous Excursion and Tours licences, operated contracts, and their coaches could often be seen at weekends on hire to large company operators. Tickets were originally Bell Punch, but in 1958 TIMs came into use. Driver-only operation was confined to quiet journeys and duplicates and in this case Setright machines were used.

Ernest Parish died in 1957, and Edgar Whittaker became Managing Director. When he decided to retire the business became the first of the local independents to sell to the PTE, in April 1976. The 15 smartly kept buses and a Land Rover were transferred to the Doncaster depot in Leicester Avenue and the Felix premises sold.

H Wilson Ltd

Harold Wilson's Premier was a pioneer operation, probably the first, to work on the Doncaster - Thorne Moorends route. Apart from a Sunday service from Hatfield to the Catholic Church in Stainforth, joint with Felix, Severn and Morgan & Store, it never ran to Stainforth, despite its premises remaining in East Lane for the whole of its 68 years' existence. Until the years following the Second World War it remained a small concern, with usually about five vehicles. The departure of the elderly ex-Leeds Guy in 1950 and two Leyland Lions the subsequent year cleared out all prewar stock. The wartime Guy Arab seems to have impressed, just as it did with Morgan and Store, and its successors became Wilson's double-decker of choice until the end of the halfcab era. Three Arab Mark IIIs, with NCB, Barnaby or Guy bodies were followed by four of the Mark IV variety: three Roe bodied and one comparative rarity with a Guy body came in the 1950s. Interesting coaches were a TSM K6LA7 and a Foden. In addition came a Guy

Arab UF, an AEC Reliance, a Bedford SB1, a Thames Trader and a 13-seat Trojan, which was replaced by another Trojan after just a year in the fleet.

By this time Harold Wilson's two sons, Don and Bob, were involved in the business and, jointly with Morgan, Store and the Corporation, it became part of the round the clock operation taking colliers from Thorne Moorends to the various mines in the area. Premier also undertook a weekday works service from Moorends to Lysaughts Steel Works in Scunthorpe. From 1960 onwards the fleet expanded rapidly with both new and second-hand acquisitions. In the 1960s alone 49 buses and coaches joined the fleet, together with three Bedfords taken over with the coaching interests of Majestic (Hopley & Richardson) of Thorne and four more Bedfords with the business of V G Aldred of Hatfield Woodhouse. There were Bedford coaches of all sizes from a little J2SZ10 to three VALs and a pair of Fords, mostly bought new. Second-hand purchases included AECs, Leylands, Maudslays and two ex-Eastern Counties Duple-bodied Bedford SBs with Gardner 4LK engines. Most of these departed after only a few years. The only notable double-deck purchase in this period was HYG 123C in 1965, a Roe bodied Daimler CRG6LX, which for a while ran experimentally with single rear tyres. Don Wilson was tragically killed in an accident in the garage, leaving the firm to be run by Bob and his mother Gina (Ernest Parish's cousin).

In the next decade a further large selection of Bedfords and Fords arrived and, after a few years, departed. With the wholesale closure of collieries the works services gradually ran down in the 1980s. One noteworthy bus was an AEC Reliance with Plaxton Derwent body and 3+2 seating, a remarkable performer. The writer recalls a motorway journey on a tour at over 80 mph and the astonished faces of car drivers as what was ostensibly a service bus overtook them at speed. It is still in the Yorkshire-based fleet of Thornes at the time of writing. Two Volvo B58s added variety to the coaching operations.

An Alexander-bodied Atlantean arrived in 1973, followed by the first second-hand double-deckers for 33 years: an AEC

Above: Harold Wilson's Daimler Fleetline *HYG 123C* is shown on a visit to West Riding's headquarters in Wakefield. Roe-bodied, it was new in October 1965.

Below: The end of Hopley & Richardson's Majestic operation came when their coaching activities were sold to Harold Wilson. This was their coach fleet taken on 1st February 1964 when the three Bedfords had just been driven to Premier's Stainforth premises. All were Bedford SBGs. **PVO 958** and **FDB 404** were sold fairly quickly to Coopers of Annitsford, but **MNB 717**, a 7ft 6ins-wide example, new in 1951, stayed with Premier until 1970.

Bridgemaster, which originated in Oxford, and an AEC Regent V from Sheffield. A very interesting addition, brand new this time, was an Alexander-bodied Volvo Ailsa B55-10, most unusual for an independent, which after several subsequent owners, spent several years in the Wallace Arnold fleet.

Originally dark blue and cream, the livery varied over the years. There were light-blue and cream vehicles, then some in two shades of blue with cream, and later a touch of bright red was added to this. Tickets were the usual Bell Punch, replaced by the Setright Speed system in 1961.

Premier had been one of the first concerns to work north-east of Doncaster and was also the last, selling out to South Yorkshire Transport in June 1988 and affording it the monopoly position it had always worked towards. All the vehicles: three Atlanteans, a Bristol VR, an Ailsa B55, two Leyand Leopards, one Ford and three Bedfords, were taken into South Yorkshire Transport's stock and at least the Atlanteans were operated.

E R Dodd

The one that almost everybody forgot about is Selwyn Motors. E R Dodd began his Saturday market express service from Belton and Epworth in 1935. The route passed the wartime aerodrome at Sandtoft, and Selwyn began to provide a daily service. A four days a week route between Belton and Thorne was also begun. The fleet was elderly in 1950, with the exception of a Bedford OB bus and a Myers & Bowman-bodied Commer Commando. There was an ex-Burton prewar Guy, the rebodied AEC Regal 4 which began life with Reading Corporation and an ex-Felix Leyland LT1. Added in that year was a positively ancient AEC Regal (chassis number 662007) from Bath Tramways. Another ex-Burton Guy followed and in 1953 an AEC Regal Burlingham appeared, together with a Duple-bodied Bedford OB which was often found on the Thorne service. When it was withdrawn in 1971 its veteran, long-service driver retired with it. Mr Dodd himself was killed in an unfortunate accident in his garage in 1955 and the owners became Mrs Queenie Dodd and Mr Donald Lindsey. Later, ownership passed to

Mrs Q and Mr B S Dodd. After the closure of Sandtoft as an aerodrome the service reverted to Saturdays only. A Bedford SBO was followed by a fully fronted AEC Regal in the early 1960s. Then came a Plaxton-bodied Tiger Cub and two AEC Reliances with Burlingham and Plaxton bodies respectively. In 1978 the first double-decker appeared in the form of an ex-North Western Alexander-bodied Daimler Fleetline. This was replaced by former London DMS 2138, which in its turn has given way to a Mark II Metrobus from MTL. The DMS languishes in the yard, in company with an AEC Reliance coach which has itself been supplanted by a Volvo. The original livery was grey and red, but more recently it has become a smart grey and ivory.

OPERATORS SOUTH OF DONCASTER

John H Barras Ltd

One of the three partners who set up Ribble Motor Services by the purchase of James Hodson's business in 1919 was John Hubert Barras. About a year later a dispute led to Barras resigning and he returned to his native Yorkshire. He began a service between Doncaster and Rossington in 1921, adopting the fleetname Don Motors, and this remained his staple route for the whole of the firm's existence, although private hire work was also undertaken. Colours were always red with cream reliefs. His prewar fleet was virtually intact in 1950, the year in which his 1932 Leyland TS4 was sent to Strachans for a new coach body. In this form it completed 27 years of service before being written off after an accident in 1959. A Leyland TS7 and a TS8 were also active, as was the 1939 Allsop-bodied Leyland Cheetah LZ4. VU 3645, the ex-Manchester Crossley Condor with the Perkins P6 engine didn't survive the year, being replaced by another Crossley, a DD42/3 bought from Brown of Garelochhead. Mr Barras liked his Leylands, and his Leyland-bodied PD1 had been new in 1947. His flagship was VDT 94, a PD2 with Burlingham body new in 1956, but he later purchased a Bristol K6A from Maidstone & District. The prewar Leylands were all withdrawn in the mid to late 1950s, making this an all double-deck fleet.

Above: This Burlingham-bodied Bedford SBO, **JVD 700**, had recently arrived with Dodd from Kerr & Smith of Coatbridge when pictured at Christ Church in April 1961. The paper label in the windscreen reads "Sandtoft, Epworth & Belton".

Below: Don Motors' last purchase was this Bristol K6A with Weymann body from Maidstone & District in 1959. **HKR 41** passed to East Midland in 1962 but was not used by them.

Wishing to retire, Barras began negotiations to sell the business to one of the other independents on the route. The scheme foundered at the last minute and, to the surprise of many, East Midland bought the company in April 1962. They took the three double-deckers, but the PD1 and the Bristol were not used. The PD2 Titan VDT 94 fitted nicely into East Midland's numbering scheme as D94.

G H Ennifer Ltd

The earlier story of G H Ennifer Ltd (Blue Ensign) is a complex and intriguing one, covered in some detail in volume one. Postwar there was considerable expansion of the private hire and excursion business. Already four coaches, two Crossley SD42s, a Maudslay Marathon 3 and an AEC Regal III had joined the fleet by 1950, with the three prewar AECs being sold in 1950/1. Service requirements were covered by the ex-London Transport Q4, which lasted until December 1951, and the Scottish Commercial-bodied Crossley DD42/5. The appropriately registered AEC Regent BUS 106 came from Glasgow to replace the Q, and three AEC Regal IV Burlingham Seagulls arrived to help develop the coaching side.

A notable purchase in 1955 was KDT 393, an AEC Regent III that had been new to Doncaster Corporation in 1951. At that time Doncaster decided that it had no use for 8ft-wide buses so, together with a Daimler CVD6 fitted with similar Roe bodywork, it was sold and Blue Ensign became its proud owner. It later passed to Tony Peart, who has lovingly restored it in Doncaster colours, and it is very active on the rally scene. The author's personal view is that, since it spent just four years with Doncaster and twelve with Blue Ensign, Tony has restored it in the wrong livery. It should have been painted in that pleasant light blue and cream, with lettering in gold. Tony disagrees; he feels the dignified Doncaster scheme suits it better, and anyway he says he couldn't afford all the gold leaf.

The business had largely been financed by Ernest Auld Heath, and on his death in 1940 his widow, Mrs B L Heath, inherited his interest. Her brother, Vernon Packer, managed the company, and his wife, Florence A Packer, became a director. The garage premises in

Bentinck Street, originally rented, had been bought, but in 1968 a move was made to fresh premises at 5 Union Street, still in the heart of the town. Ultimate tickets were adopted in 1956, but a change was made in 1957 to the Setright system.

The heavyweight era came to an end with a succession of Bedford coaches from 1957 onwards. No fewer than 17 were bought new, but it was rare for more than three or four to be in the fleet at any one time. Two magnificent Roe-bodied AEC Regent Vs, always kept in the smartest condition, ran on the Rossington route. In poor weather when the service bus became dirty, it was often taken out of service for one trip and replaced with another one while it was washed. The first Daimler Fleetline arrived in 1967, and in 1975 both the Regent Vs were replaced by two further Roe-bodied CRG6LX Fleetlines.

In 1971 the company title was changed to Blue Ensign Coaches Ltd. It passed to South Yorkshire PTE in April 1978, with the three Daimler Fleetlines and three Bedford coaches, all of which stayed in the PTE fleet for several years. It is reported that the driver on the last Blue Ensign journey, the long-serving Jack Fretwell, a man who knew every pothole and grid cover on the way to Rossington, was instructed to take his bus into the PTE depot at Leicester Avenue. He refused: "This bus goes back to Union Street, where it's always gone".

Rossie Motors Ltd

William Morpus started the Rossie undertaking in 1923. From 1930 onwards he had favoured Daimlers, a trait which continued until the very end of the firm's existence. His principal service was between Doncaster and his base, Rossington, though he held an interesting express licence from Doncaster to Wrexham, presumably for miners and their families emanating from Wales, together with a number of excursion and tours licences.

The fleet in 1950 consisted of FV 1003, a twice-rebodied Daimler CF6 with Perkins engine, a wartime Bedford OWB, a Daimler CP6 double-decker from Kingston upon Hull Corporation, three Daimler CVD6 single-deckers - two coaches and one with a bus body - and a Barnard-bodied CVD6 double-decker.

Above: The happily registered **BUS 106** came from Glasgow in December 1951. A Weymann-bodied 1938 AEC Regent, it is shown in Waterdale. It was 22 years old when withdrawn in 1960.

Below: Seen parked in Chequer Road, Doncaster, **MWU 750** was bought by Rossie in 1953. It had an experimental Daimler CD650 chassis, and was exhibited at the Festival of Britain in 1951 with a well-appointed Burlingham body. After chassis modifications it became a demonstrator before passing to Rossie. *(James Firth)*

Colours were green & ivory, with some vehicles in two shades of green, dark and light, together with the ivory. In 1951 the English Electric body from RH 6118, the ex-Hull Daimler CP6, was transferred to a brand new Daimler CVD6 chassis. Three years later this bus gained a new Burlingham double-deck body of apparently an earlier design, the origins of which have been the subject of some controversy.

A Burlingham-bodied experimental Daimler CD650 chassis was exhibited at the Festival of Britain in 1951, and subsequently served as a demonstrator after having had modifications to the chassis. Rossie bought it and it entered service in August 1953. Although it served for 16 years, was lavishly finished inside, and on withdrawal donated its engine to Tailby & George (Blue Bus), it was never a favourite. "It only does the same work as the others, yet uses more fuel" was the verdict, and the power steering was removed as troublesome. When Doncaster was shedding its lowbridge deckers, Rossie bought GDT 421, a CVD6. This was sold for preservation in 1971, and resides at present at Sandtoft. As happened at Blue Ensign, new Bedford coaches were bought, 15 in all, none residing in the fleet for more than five years. The last two, a pair of Caetano bodied YLQs, were sold in 1975 to Beehive Services of Adwick le Street, together with the licences for the Wrexham service and Rossie's excursions and tours licences.

William Morpus died in 1962, and his daughter and her husband, Mr & Mrs Percy Doxey, took over the reins. The first 30ft double-decker came in that year, a front-entrance Roe bodied Daimler CVD6/30; two years later a similarly bodied CVG6/30 followed.

Two ex-Southdown Leyland-bodied PD2s, intended for schools work, appeared in the mid 1960s. The final double-deckers in the fleet were a pair of Daimler CRG6LX Fleetlines and a Leyland FE30AGR (much the same thing anyway), all Roe-bodied. At first Bell Punch tickets were used, later replaced by Ultimate machines.

South Yorkshire PTE paid £90,000 for the company in May 1980. The deal included the three Fleetlines, which were used by the Executive, and the two halfcab Daimlers which were not, although 220 AWY, the CVD6/30, something of a rarity, was retained by them for preservation for a while, although it is now in Bannister's yard in Owston Ferry.

Leon Motors Ltd

Leon, with an unbroken history of over 80 years, was the longest lived of all the Doncaster independents. It was established in 1923 with a route to Finningley and Blaxton in opposition to, and after the Road Traffic Act in conjunction with, T S Madeley's Premier.

After various changes of address in the earlier days, in 1937 the company moved to the grandly named Finningley House, and some years later moved further along the same road to an ex-RAF site which offered commodious premises for the fleet. Licences were held in the name of Florence Amy Heath until the limited company was formed in January 1947. For many years colours were aquamarine (similar to the current Arriva shade) and cream, later changing slightly to what was described as Cambridge blue and broken white. The latest livery was two shades of blue with grey relief.

Essentially a rural route in the beginning, impetus came in the years leading up to the Second World War and during that war, when Finningley RAF Aerodrome became of significant national importance. Subsequently there was much housing development along the line of route.

T R Rees, the Heaths' son-in-law, became manager in April 1946, and a fleet numbering system was inaugurated.

Tom Madeley's business passed to Leon on his retirement in December 1950, and with it Leon added to its fleet six vehicles which became fleet numbers 21-6: an elderly Leyland TS1, a Bedford OWB, a remarkable old Crossley Condor with a Perkins engine and an Atkinson lorry radiator, an ex-Birmingham Guy Arab II and two nearly new Strachan-bodied Crossley coaches.

Leon's own fleet in 1950 comprised the unique centre-entrance Leyland Lion LT5a double-decker, soon to be scrapped, a Leyland TS1 rebodied as a Plaxton coach, an ex-Bury Daimler CP6 with two staircases and a Leyland engine, three AEC Regents and a Regal from Halifax, two Bedford OWBs, and six coaches,

Above: The chassis of this Daimler CD650/30 had been a Commercial Motor Show exhibit when new in 1958. It was fitted with a Roe front-entrance body, registered **432 KAL**, and entered service as Leon **57** in July 1961.

Below: Leon favoured Bedford VAL14 service buses for a time. **ARR 720B**, with its Duple Midland body, was almost new when photographed on a snowy day in December 1964.

all but one bought new: two Bedford OBs and four Daimler CVD6s. The excursion and tours business was taken very seriously; several useful licences were held, and there was a thriving private hire connection.

This situation continued in the 1950s when four Bedford SBGs arrived and also a Burlingham Seagull-bodied Daimler Freeline D650H. There was an intriguing Willowbrook-bodied bus, FRW 587, which had an experimental CVD6 chassis and was originally Daimler works transport. Double-deckers came and went: two more Regents, from Salford this time; London contributed an STL, an RT and three Daimler CWA6s; and from Rochdale there were two Massey-bodied Daimlers, a CWD6 and a CWA6. FBW 887, which was a rather nice CVD6 with platform doors. Another CVD6 which stayed for 14 years was KDT 392, the second of the 8ft-wide buses sold by Doncaster Corporation in 1953.

The following decade saw an even greater influx of stock. Coaching gained six Bedford SBs, a VAM, two VALs and two more CVD6s, while the bus fleet saw a turnover of a CWD6, three Roberts-bodied CVD6s from Leicester, a Leyland PD2, three ex-Devon General AEC Regent IIIs and a pair of Regent Vs from Oxford. One double-decker was bought new, a front-entrance Roe-bodied Daimler CD650/30, and a Duple Midland-bodied Bedford VAL bus was also new. Later two more similar VALs, but with Willowbrook bodies, came from Wigmores of Dinnington.

Seven Bedford coaches, almost all new, joined the fleet in the 1970s, but the years following saw just one more Bedford, then a Leyland Leopard and a couple of Tigers. Daimler and then Leyland Fleetlines arrived, new ones coming in 1972/3/5/8/80, and a second-hand one in 1976 plus a couple of second-hand Atlanteans. An unusual venture was No. 93, a Ford minibus with Asco body and tail lift, used as a community bus.

For many years the pattern of services had changed little. In 1979 Leon's licences were:

Doncaster to Finningley (daily, with some journeys extended to Wroot on Tuesdays and Saturdays);
Doncaster to Misson (daily);
Finningley to Auckley schools service;

Doncaster to Great Yarmouth summer express;
Lindholme (RAF Station) to Derby special occasions express;
Finningley (RAF Station) to Manchester special occasions express;
Excursions and tours from Doncaster (three groups) and Finningley.

A spending spree with South Yorkshire PTE in the early 1980s resulted in five Fleetlines arriving which had come from Doncaster independents, two from Felix and three from Rossie.

Leon had long been involved with schools transport, but following deregulation there was a massive expansion in stage services. The initial venture was the Doncaster Inner Circle route in October 1986, for which two Mercedes minibuses were bought. This later passed to Yorkshire Traction. A group of subsidised services in the Stainforth and Thorne area began in 1987, for which three Leyland Cubs came from West Yorkshire PTE. These were either lost or faded away, though the Doncaster to Sykehouse route reverted to Leon and was still operative at the time of writing. Leon also ran about nine tendered Sunday and/or evening services in the late 1980s, but none remain with Leon, if still running, which is doubtful. An interesting service was Haxey to Scunthorpe, with one journey a day extended to Doncaster, which began in 1991. Two Leyland Lynxes obtained from Southampton ran the route, which ended in 1999.

The final tally of Leon's operations was:

Doncaster to Finningley (begun in 1922; the Wroot service passed to Wilfreda-Beehive in 2001);
Doncaster to Warmsworth (begun in 1991);
Doncaster to Hexthorpe (begun in 1991);
Doncaster to Askern, acquired from Retford & District December 1995;
Doncaster to Sykehouse, acquired from Retford & District December 1995;
Misson to Retford (begun in 2001).

In this period no fewer than 15 Daimler/Leyland Fleetlines and seven Leyland Atlanteans came and went, sourced from Yorkshire Rider, West Midland, South

Above: Seen here in Finningley, Leon **84** was a Roe bodied Daimler CRL6/30, **SNN 5L**, purchased new in 1972.

Below: After deregulation Leon expanded its sphere of operation. **P877 PWW**, a Dennis Dart SLF, was on service in Retford in August 2001.

Yorkshire, and Greater Manchester PTEs, Clydeside, Western Scottish and Dodds (AA). All these have now departed, to be replaced by nine Leyland Olympians acquired from, among others, Cardiff, Go Coastline and Arriva. Two brand new East Lancs-bodied Dennis Tridents joined the fleet in July 2000. Further Dennises are three Darts, one new and two second-hand; four Optare Metroriders, all new, are also in stock. The same period saw the coach fleet equipped with seven more Leyland Tigers, a Royal Tiger and a DAF.

The Leon story ended on a sad note. The business was sold in February 2004 to MASS Special Engineering of North Anston. Only a few months later came the death of Tony Rees, the grandson of founders Leonard and Florence Heath, and the astute, hands-on manager of the company for many years.

OTHER OPERATORS

After deregulation several concerns not previously involved in stage-carriage work decided to try their hands at bus operation. The most significant of these was Wilfreda-Beehive, a firm which merits a place among the traditional Doncaster independents.

E A Hart commenced operations early in World War Two with an elderly Gilford, to which he added a Bedford OWB and four buses bought from Doncaster Corporation, in order to run a group of works services. Later he added another OWB and five ancient vehicles, three ex-Rotherham Bristol Bs and a couple of Tilling-Stevens B10A2s from West Yorkshire Road Car Company.

A new chapter opened in 1947 when the Doncaster Co-operative Society bought an interest, and new capital brought in six new Daimler CVD6s (most with Yorkshire Equipment bodies built in Bridlington) and several more second-hand vehicles. The title of Beehive Services was adopted. Mr Hart left the company in early 1948, and set up Kildare Coaches just around the corner from the premises in Adwick le Street.

In the years which followed, many new coaches were added, mostly Bedfords, and the Yorkshire Equipment Daimlers received new Duple bodies similar to the pattern then being fitted to Bedford SBs. There was a noteworthy batch of four Foden PVREs, with two-stroke rear engines, and fitted with Whitson bodies. Colours were dark green and cream, and vehicles were smartly kept, as befitted a firm with a substantial private hire connection with excursion licences from Carcroft and Adwick. By 1952 eleven licences for works services were held, plus some for football matches.

In 1975 Beehive bought the licences for the Doncaster to Wrexham express service and their Excursion & Tours licences from Rossie Motors, together with two Caetano-bodied Bedford YLQs.

Wilfreda of Ranskill purchased the Beehive operation in August 1987, and Wilfreda Luxury Coaches Ltd moved their headquarters to Apex House, Church Lane, Adwick le Street, with the joint operation trading as Wilfreda-Beehive. To Wilfreda's very mixed fleet, Beehive brought ten Bedfords and three DAFs.

It moved into bus operation in quite a big way, particularly in the early 1990s, registering at various times some 14 commercial services, many of which paralleled existing routes, including Doncaster town services to Beckett Road and Lothian Road, and such routes as Skellow, Scawthorpe, Cantley, Woodlands, Armthorpe, Barnby Dun, Edlington, West Bessacarr and also to Rotherham in the evenings. There was a number of tendered services, mostly evenings, off-peak or Sundays. To work these routes, in addition to four Fleetlines, eight Leyland Nationals were acquired from Bristol, and a couple of minibuses. At the same time a range of extended tour destinations was built up, and for these new coaches were purchased, two Bovas and eight Scanias

The business of John Roe & Son of Stainforth (trading as Roeville) was purchased in July 1993. Although a relative newcomer to the bus world, John Roe was descended from one of the very earliest operators in the area, Alice Roe, and also from Walter Roe of Fishlake. With the business came an AEC Regent V which until recently was a useful recovery vehicle. The standard livery of the period was white and blue, which later became white with blue and yellow reliefs. Vehicle allocations were actually to three different firms - Wilfreda Luxury Coaches Ltd, E A Hart Ltd and Roeville Tours Ltd, all registered at the

Above: **DT 4148** began its career in 1933 as Doncaster Corporation 43, a Roe-bodied Dennis Lancet. It was sold to E A Hart in 1942 and with his other vehicles passed to Beehive Service (Doncaster Co-operative Society) in early 1948. It was sent to the Yorkshire Equipment Company in Bridlington and returned in December 1948 with its new coach body, in which guise it lasted until late 1955. It is seen here in Woodlands.

Below: Wilfreda-Beehive **V320 EAK** is shown at Hill Top, Edlington. A Scania N113DRB with East Lancs body, it was new in 1999. *(Jim Sambrooks)*

Apex House address. A small fleet of taxis, Access Taxis, has also been owned for a number of years.

In the later 1990s the company disposed of most of its bus service to Mainline, and concentrated on coaching activities with a modern fleet of mostly Scania coaches. Latterly interest in bus operation has returned. Two East Lancs Pyoneer-bodied Scanias have been joined by a steadily growing number of new Optare Solos, Dennis Darts and Mercedes minibuses to operate a group of services for the PTE. In the last five years more routes have been taken on. Some are school-related, many are evening- or Sunday-only, but there is a core of daily operations: Doncaster to Tickhill, Highfields and Wroot via Armthorpe. One or two are not Doncaster-based, such as the hourly Thorne Circular, Rotherham to Worksop, and Crystal Peaks (Sheffield) to Letwell. Recent purchases include a pair of BMC school buses. The company has also begun providing a service to the inappropriately named Robin Hood Airport (Finningley to you and me) with a new Optare Tempo, labelled the "Airport Arrow".

Immediately following deregulation Coachcraft, based in Armthorpe, began regular daytime services to Armthorpe, Cantley and Edenthorpe. This firm was associated with the coachbuilders Crystal, but after a few months the routes were discontinued. For a while in the 1990s Swift of Blaxton ran into the town, and a Saturday service from Gainsborough operated by Star Tours has also been reported.

In more recent times Isle Coaches, of Owston Ferry, have begun running supported services from Lincolnshire, and Powell's buses, based in Hellaby, are carving a niche for themselves with a number of services to the west of the town.

Upper: LYL 722, Everett's rather exotic Beccols-bodied Leyland Royal Tiger unloads returning holiday makers in Wood Street, Doncaster, in September 1963. It was working on hire to Yorkshire Traction.

Lower: County Motors of Lepton were the original owners of this Roe-bodied Guy Arab II, CCX 931, before it joined the Everett fleet. Seen in 1960, it had a further year to go before withdrawal.

Above: Once London Transport lowbridge STL 1973, **DLU 171** was another of Everett's passing parade of double-deckers. Photographed just after purchase in May 1953, it lasted only 18 months. Note the cab door.

Below: Brand new, in Wakefield bus station on its first day in service in August 1970, Cooper's Bedford VAM70 **EWX 819H** had a 51-seat Willowbrook body. Proving satisfactory, it was joined two years later by a similar vehicle, a YRQ this time.

Upper left: W R & P Bingley's double-decks were a mix of new and second-hand. Ex-Leeds Leyland TD5 **FNW 707** is seen in Wakefield in July 1953. The destination blind seems hardly adequate.

Lower left: Altogether Bingley bought a total of six ex-Ribble double-deckers, including a pair from the second batch of "White Ladies". **DCK 213** was an East Lancs-bodied Leyland PD2/3, seen here in the Upton depot yard.

Below: **LTO 10** was a well-appointed Duple-bodied Daimler CVD6 which was new to Skills of Nottingham in 1949. It passed to Bingley in 1954, was reconditioned in late 1960, as pictured here, and completed 15 years service with the company.

Above: One of a pair of Roe-bodied AEC Regent Vs delivered in 1957, **UWT 876** was a stalwart on Bingley's Doncaster to Wakefield service for many years.

Below: In the 1970s Bingley's "main line" route was largely worked by single deckers. **DWW 434H**, seen in Wakefield in 1970 when new, was one of three Leyland PSU3 Leopards with Plaxton dual-purpose bodies.

Above: Laying over in Waterdale before returning to Marshgate to pick up its return passengers, **WJU 406** was a Leyland Leopard L2. It had been a Willowbrook demonstrator before Holling bought it in January 1962.

Below: **DDW 34**, a Guy Arab I, was delivered to Newport Corporation in 1943 fitted with an MCW body which had been destined for a Manchester Daimler COG5. The Daimler factory was bombed and the chassis could not be built, so bodies already in work were requisitioned and fitted to wartime Guys. The picture was taken in May 1954. *(James Firth)*

Above: Seen in Stainforth, Blue Line **NWX 442** was a Leyland Tiger Cub with a 43 seat Mann Egerton body, new in July 1954. It was followed a year later by a Guy Arab LUF with a similar body.

Below: The first 30ft-long double-deck in the Doncaster area was **SWU 876**, which had been exhibited at the 1956 Commercial Motor Show, and entered service with Blue Line in December of that year. A Burlingham-bodied Guy Arab IV, it had a Meadows 6DC engine which was subsequently replaced with a Gardner 6LW.

Above: Not the most handsome of vehicles, despite the metallic blue finish, **UWW 769**, a Guy Warrior with Mulliner bodywork, was not popular with either drivers or mechanics. It arrived in the Blue Line fleet in December 1957, and was sold to Mosley of Barugh Green in 1961.

Below: **891 GWT** was the oldest of the Roe-bodied Guy Arab Vs in the Blue Line & Reliance operation, and the only one in serviceable condition when acquired by the PTE in1979. Its younger stablemates were all off the road for a variety of reasons, including a remarkable series of accidents. New in 1963, it was three years old when pictured in the yard at Armthorpe with that down-to-earth destination display.

Above: Blue Line snapped up the pair of Leyland PD3A/Roe double-deckers, just over two years old, when they were put on sale from the Kippax & District fleet in April 1968. Here is **DUG 166C** on its way to an Air Display in Finningley, on hire to Leon.

Below: Blue Line **230 GWR** was a Bedford VAL14 with Duple Vega Major body, that was bought new in December 1963.

Above: Local enthusiast Mike Fowler pilots Store's Bedford SB1 **6833 WY** over the narrow bridge at Barnby Dun as it makes the final journey to Kirkhouse Green in June 1971.

Below: **TYG 4**, Store's first 30ft-long double-decker came in September 1957. It was very similar to Blue Line SWU 876, but had an exposed radiator and a Gardner 6LW from new.

Above: **MNU 777**, a Guy Arab III with Northern Coachbuilders bodywork, was new in 1948. It passed to Trent when Naylors of South Normanton was taken over, and was bought by Store in 1960.

Below: Passengers are waiting to board Reliance **HWW 775J**, a Daimler Fleetline CRG6LX, bound for Goole in June 1978. Things had changed since the 5-ton weight restriction on Rawcliffe Bridge had been lifted.

Above: For a time Severn buses carried advertising for local firms. Seen at Dunscroft, Roe bodied **NWY 777** of 1954 was the last of their PD2s before regulations allowed longer double-deckers.

Below: New in 1958 , **UWU 515** was the first of seven PD3s with Roe bodies for Severn. It had just gained platform doors when photographed here in 1965, and carries the Severn garter badge. Note the Morris Minor, used almost universally by driving schools in those days.

Above: This Duple bodied Leyland Royal Tiger coach, **KWX 549**, served Severn for 21 years before being sold for use by a local school.

Below: Working the free bus service from Doncaster Station to Sandtoft Transport Centre on 31st July 1977 is Severn's **OWX 769M**. A Bedford YRQ, it had a 45-seat Plaxton body.

Above: Plaxton-bodied **PWX 591E** was a dual-purpose AEC Reliance 590 when delivered in 1967. Two years later it gained an AH691 engine, then passing to the PTE in 1979 and giving several years of further service.

Below: The only Albion Atlantean south of the Scottish border was **XWU 890G**. A Roe-bodied PDR1, it was delivered in January 1969, and was built with an order for Glasgow.

Severn bought ex-London RT 331 (**HLX 148**) in October 1963, selling it 18 months later to a Bingo Hall in Batley.

Above: **YYG 649G**, the first Felix Daimler Fleetline, came in May 1969. Shown here when new, it was the only dual-door rear-engined double-decker owned by any Doncaster independent.

Below: Felix **44** (**493 DWW**), an AEC Reliance with Duple coachwork, was six years old in this picture and typified the smart condition of the fleet.

Above: This Roe Dalesman-bodied AEC Reliance, Felix No. **40** (**XWX 795**), is seen returning to Doncaster from Blackpool in July 1960. *(James Firth)*

Below: Photographed in May 1969, **9629 WU**, an AEC Reliance, carried a Roe dual-purpose body. It survives in preservation, though with a different livery style.

Above: Premier's **MWW 891**, seen here in June 1954, was one of the few Guy Arab IVs to carry a Guy body.

Below: It was Premier's policy to have several different sizes of coach in the fleet. **JYG 538D** was a neat little 20-seat Plaxton-bodied Bedford J2SZ10.

Above: In the 1960s and 70s Premier added a touch of red to their two-tone blue and cream. **HUM 951N**, seen here in 1971, was the speedy AEC Reliance Plaxton-bodied bus mentioned earlier, which was latterly in the Thornes fleet. Decimalisation had come in on 15th February 1971 and it is rather poignant to see petrol at less per gallon than it now is per litre.

Below: In the early 1960s the company bought three of the Yeates front-entrance conversions of the Bedford SB5, more modern in style than the original Pegasus concept. **888 CWY**, new in 1964, was the third of the trio.

Above: Premier were also customers for the Leyland AN68. **XWU 798L**, an Alexander-bodied example, was new in May 1973.

Below: After many years of buying Bedford coaches, for a time in the 1970s Fords were Premier's choice. **CWU 185H** was one of a pair of Plaxton-bodied buses.

Above: Premier's purchasing policy took an out of character turn in 1973, when two well-travelled AECs were acquired. 7871 WJ was a Regent V that had been new to Sheffield, and there was also this ex-City of Oxford Bridgemaster, **310 MFC**.

Below: E R Dodd's Selwyn Motors has owned a succession of AEC Reliance coaches over the years, the first one being their Duple-bodied example, **571 BWT**, which the firm acquired in June 1969.

Above: AEC Regent III **KDT 393**, an 8ft-wide vehicle, was new to Doncaster Corporation in 1951. Four years later it was deemed too wide for Doncaster's streets and was sold to Blue Ensign, who kept it for twelve years before selling it to a driving school. It was rescued by Tony Peart and lovingly restored into its original livery. The Corporation destination blind appears to have travelled with it.

Below: **ODT 845**, new in 1954, was the third of the Blue Ensign AEC Regal IVs with Burlingham Seagull bodies. Next to it is Leon's **EF 7939**, a centre-entrance Daimler CVD6 ex-West Hartlepool Corporation.

Above: Blue Ensign replaced their heavyweight coaches with a trio of Bedford SB5s in 1961, and all subsequent coaches were Bedfords. **8971 DT** is seen in the yard in May 1965.

Below: The last double-deckers delivered to Blue Ensign were two Daimler CRG6LX Fleetlines in 1975. This is **JAK 926M**.

Above: Rossie's **KWT 600** entered service in April 1951 with the 1934 English Electric body from their ex-Hull Corporation Daimler CP6 RH 6118.

Below: In November 1954, **KWT 600** was rebodied with this Burlingham body, apparently new although of an earlier design.

Above: Rossie was another convert to Bedford coaches. **KWR 510D** was a VAM5, new in 1966, pictured here in 1970 just before it was sold on.

Below: **TKU 562** was a Bedford SB1 new in 1960, and fitted with the none too happily styled Burlingham Seagull 60 body.

Above: Leon's No. **47** (**HLW 142**) was ex-London Transport RT155, which arrived in 1958 and was a useful member of the fleet for eight years.

Above: Massey-bodied **FBW 887** was this attractive Daimler CVD6, Leon No. **48**, which came from Ronsway in Hemel Hempstead in 1958. Behind it is No. **41**, another Massey-bodied vehicle, on a Daimler CWA6 chassis that had been new to Rochdale Corporation.

Below: Seen in Waterdale is **PNN 788**, Leon's 1954 Daimler Freeline fitted with a Burlingham Seagull body.

Above: Doncaster Corporation had another 8ft-wide bus in addition to the AEC Regent already mentioned as having been sold to Blue Ensign. This was **KDT 392**, a Daimler CVD6 with a similar Roe "Pullman" body. When Doncaster decided that 8ft-wide buses were not a success, the Daimler was sold to Leon as their No. **39** in November 1955.

Below: Leon had numerous Bedford coaches, some bought new, some second-hand. Fleet number **56** (**XTJ 275**) was an SBG model with Plaxton coachwork, which came from Wingate Tours in 1960.

Upper: Devon General was the source of three Weymann-bodied AEC Regent IIIs. As Leon No. **67**, **PDV 725** is seen in Finningley shortly after delivery in August 1966.

Centre: Leon's Alexander-bodied Daimler Fleetline (badged as a Leyland) **HKU 361W** looks very smart in this July 1982 picture, also taken in Finningley.

Lower: This Asco-bodied Ford 20-seat minibus, No. **93 UWB 189S**, new in May 1978, was operated by Leon as the Bassetlaw Community Bus. This is a May 1979 photograph. *(Geoff Coxon)*

Upper: An impressive line of nine assorted double-deckers posed in the depot yard for Leon's 60th Anniversary photograph. *(Jim Sambrooks)*

Centre: Leon's No. **131** (**F103 RTR**), a Leyland Lynx, was acquired from Southampton in 1991 and this picture of it was taken in May 1992. *(Geoff Coxon)*

Lower: Leon No. **127** (**GDZ 885**), a Leyland Tiger with Van Hool coachwork was acquired second-hand from Travellers, Hounslow. It is seen here in September 2001 at Duxford, having brought a party to the annual Showbus event.

Upper: KWU 26, seen here in May 1954, was one of four Whitson-bodied Foden PVREs new to Beehive in 1951. All later saw further service with other firms.

Centre: During Wilfreda-Beehive's expansionist period, Leyland Cub CU435 **C923 DKR**, which had a 33-seat HTI-Maxeta body, was photographed in Pipering Lane, Scawthorpe. The 1983 vehicle had been acquired from the Dartford, Kent, operator Springham in 1989. *(Jim Sambrooks)*

Lower: PJI 5017 was originally a 1975 Leyland National, GEU 361N, of the Bristol Omnibus Company Ltd. It passed to Wilfreda Beehive in late 1990. Always a dual-door 44-seater, it was rebuilt by East Lancs as a Greenway, to the same layout but with a welfare lift, in January 1993; at the same time it was reregistered as shown. It was photographed in June 1994 leaving Doncaster for Scawthorpe. *(Geoff Coxon)*